T0107417

About the Author

Terry was born in Little Rock, AR in 1954, the son of Tommy and Virginia Trent. His awareness of the Spirit of the Father in his life goes back into his childhood for as long as he can remember. At age 11 he joined a church and was Baptized, and has been involved in varying degrees with church attendance ever since.

"There were times in stages of my life that my walk went with the flow of the world as most people do, but truly I never lost sight of my core belief. I hope that others who may be believers in Jesus Christ may benefit from my years of research into the restoration of the Holy Bible. A GRAND AWAKENING is on the horizon."

- Terry N. Trent, Sr.

authorHOUSE

AuthorHouse™
1663 Liberty Drive
Bloomington, IN 47403
www.authorhouse.com
Phone: 833-262-8899

Published by AuthorHouse 10/11/2023

ISBN: 979-8-8230-1298-0 (sc)
ISBN: 979-8-8230-1297-3 (e)

Library of Congress Control Number: 2023914941

This story begins in the year 5 A. D. as Saul was born in the city of Tarsus in Cilica, an area today we know as Turkey, to Jewish parents who were Roman citizens. That coveted privilege of Roman citizenship extended to Saul, and when he was 5 years of age his family moved to Jerusalem. Early in his life he did not believe in any of the teachings of Christ. Then in his teen years he reportedly began to study the Hebrew Scriptures under the rabbi Gamaliel, and soon he picked up studies in law as well. It is said in much of the internet info that is available that Saul/Paul became a Christian apostle who spread the teachings of Jesus in the first-century, post ascension world. This, of course is only after his trip to Damascus where he supposedly "SAW THE LIGHT", so to speak. He may well have seen a light, but as we check his writings and his history, you may begin to wonder about the source of this light. The strange difference in his teachings when compared to those of Christ will have you wondering where did the short-circuit occur, OR... is the intention there to CHANGE the direction of the Christian church? Read on and decide for yourself.

One of the earliest episodes of note in the adult life of Saul/Paul was the tale of his presence at the stoning of Stephen, the first Christian martyr. In Acts 7:58, Luke tells us that those who killed Stephen laid their garments at the feet of Saul who was in full agreement and approval with this killing. And as for Saul himself, he made havock of the church, entering into every house, terrorizing men and women and dragging them off to prison. His anti-Christian attitude motivated him to lock up the women just the same as the men in his rampage (Acts 8:1-3). Saul was a self-admitted Jew and also referred to himself and his father as Pharisees.

By definition, a Pharisee is a Jewish secretary, and Saul certainly was well educated for that. The writings he and those around him so carefully planned and produced are some carefully crafted "word salads", which in many cases are very hard for many of his day and even nowadays to fully understand. In some cases, that would be because the thoughts actually do not connect or make any kind of good sense. Possibly one prime illustration of this purposeful confusion is the opening SENTENCE of Hebrews which covers 4 verses and contains TWELVE punctuation marks. It reads... *"God, who at sundry times and in divers manners spake in time past unto the fathers by the prophets, Hath in these last days spoken unto us by his Son, whom he hath appointed heir of all things, by whom also he made the worlds; Who being the brightness of his glory, and the express image of his person, and upholding all things by the word of his power, when he had by himself purged our sins, sat down on the right hand of the Majesty on high; Being made so much better than the angels, as he hath by inheritance obtained a more excellent name than they."* Yes, this proclaims a glorious message of how The Father once used the prophets to bring His Word to His people, and then Christ came on to assume those duties until He returned to the Father with a proven reputation far above the angels. I get it. But just how many phrases heaped upon phrases should one need to endure in consecutive fashion like that to get this message understood. I dare say many would argue that my paraphrasing of that passage may be less than accurate, and due to the nature of all that is packed into that rant, I would agree that rather than paraphrasing, the whole thing would be made much better by just simply rewriting it to be more easily understood by all readers and be done with it. That is exactly the point. Many times Paul's language IS the disguise and is rooted in deceit. A big part of the deceit in this passage is the CONSTANT theme used by Paul to make completely separate the image of the Father and the Son, rather than to acknowledge the fact that CHRIST WAS GOD IN THE FLESH, and as Christ said in John 10:30... ***"I and my Father are one"***.

When you actually compare (on your own) the teachings of Paul with the teachings of Christ, you will no doubt be able to see that they are nowhere near the same. Christ told His disciples in Matthew 10:5,6... *These twelve Jesus sent forth, and commanded them,*

2

saying, **"Go not into the way of the Gentiles** (Correctly defined, Gentiles means any nation or race other than your own, in this case, go not to any nation or race other than the descendants or family of Jacob, a man who was renamed Israel by God)**, and into any city of the Samaritans enter ye not: But go rather to the lost sheep of the house** (family) **of Israel** (Jacob)**."** You should compare that solid and unwaivering instruction from Christ with the "gospel" Paul declares to be his interpretation of that Gospel of Christ found in Romans 1:16... *"For I am not ashamed of the gospel of Christ: for it is the power of God unto salvation to every one that believeth; to the Jew first, and also to the Greek."* Not even close. Notice the deceit in saying he is not ashamed of the Gospel of Christ, and then as if he is declaring to restate just what that Gospel of Christ is... he instead inserts his own UNIVERSAL doctrine to not only rebuke the fact that the Gospel is meant exclusively for the house of Israel, but also to say that the Jew is now to be included, FURTHERMORE to also be saying that it is for the JEW FIRST... ding, ding... is anybody listening to what this Jewish secretary is saying? This may well be the world's first official move towards the NEW WORLD ORDER! An order for placing the JEW FIRST... and in complete control of everything.

Another instance of variance we will find presented by Paul is in Romans 10:4... *"For Christ is the end of the law for righteousness to every one that believeth."* A complete reversal to the determination by Christ as to how long you may expect the Law to remain in place. That is found in Matthew 5:18... **"For verily I say unto you, Till heaven and earth pass, one jot or one tittle shall in no wise pass from the law, till all be fulfilled."** There are those who want to make issue about the final part of that statement, interpreting that **"till all be fulfilled"** refers to the finished work of Christ's Death and Resurrection as a total and complete fulfillment of the Law of God. That is an undeniable stretch and actually a "bridge

3

too far" when you note Christ saying in the beginning of this statement, *"For verily I say unto you, Till heaven and earth pass..."* and I am pretty sure we can ALL agree that heaven and earth HAVE NOT PASSED as of the Death and Resurrection, or even until right now, for that matter. And that has to mean He meant something else with those final words of the statement or else that creates a contradiction within the sentence. So obviously, the reference of TILL ALL BE FULFILLED is instead a reference to a time at the end of the age, when EVERYTHING WILL BE FULFILLED for sure, with the return of Jesus Christ and His angels to carry out the details outlined in the book of Revelation.

There is a writing by the Imposter Paul which truly begins to smell like something very foul, found in 1 Corinthians 4:15-16... *"For though ye have ten thousand instructors in Christ, yet have ye not many fathers: for in Christ Jesus I have begotten you through the gospel. Wherefore I beseech you, be ye followers of me."* With that bit about "I have begotten you" (become your father), and then also saying THROUGH the Gospel, Paul is often using vague terms to cloud the meaning of a statement he is making. And the worst of all in this smelly scripture is the idea that, as Paul says... "ye be followers of ME." Gag me with a dead sea scoll! This is a wanna-be-GOD... not just an apostle. And anyway, if Paul has begotten anyone, Christ has told us for sure to "call no man your father upon the earth: for one is your Father, which is in heaven." that found in Matthew 23:9. This may be where Paul misled the Catholic church into a bad habit of referring to their priests as "father". Many will say that Paul merely meant to be saying follow me as I follow Christ. If that were the case, it would have been easy to just say that instead. But this is exactly why Paul lays a statement out there that can go either of two ways. This is the practice of some very sublte deceit. Look at Chapter 1 in Romans, a word salad sentence covering SEVEN verses using 21 punctuation marks! And embedded in that we see in verse 4... *"And declared to be the Son of God with power, according to the spirit of holiness, by the resurrection from the dead:"* Now let us simplify that statement even further: ...declared to be the Son of God by the resurrection of the dead. Regardless of Paul's intentions, what that actually says is... the death and resurrection is what made Christ the Son of God. And that means Paul says that throughout Christ's life here on earth, He was NOT GOD, but merely a mortal man, the fleshly seed of David (An Israelite of the 12 Tribes). It is true that the mother of Christ descended from David. And here it is important to note: the error of this thinking is that the truth of the matter is GOD VISITED HIS PEOPLE in the fleshly form of Jesus Christ without ANY regard for the Death and Resurrection, at all. That fact backed up by assorted passages including Psalms 8:4. In that passage "son of man" refers to the Adamic race. That is who God visited in the flesh.

Translators were also Paul's partners-in-crime with many passages in the early scriptures such as Psalms 8:4 where the word "man" is used twice to hide the fact that two completely different words were replaced by the one same word man! *"What is man, that thou art mindful of him? and the son of man, that thou visitest him?"* The first mention of man had been the word "ENOSH", a reference to mortal man of wicked character, wretchedness. These men are of the 6th day creation of men and women God had told to be fruitful and multiply, and REPLENISH the earth. (Replenish being another word replaced by translators in ALL Bibles printed since the KJV in an attempt to hide the fact that there was an age which existed BEFORE Genesis; see Jeremiah 4:23-27). But back to Psalms 8:4, the second usage of the word man in that verse replaced the original word AWDAWM... a refence to the descendants of Adam and Eve created after the 7 days were finshed and Blessed. So in the final analysis of this verse, we learn that GOD VISITED ADAM'S RACE in the person of Jesus Christ, while also keeping an eye on those men of wicked character who were created on the 6th day and

5

mentioned at the start of Gen. 2 as the "HOST" (masses of people).

This kind of verse rigging is why we all now must rethink so much of what we thought we knew, but were fooled by translators and their "rock star" wanna-be-apostle Paul. These most subtle creatures are masters of deception, and understandably so when you consider their origin. Most who will try and defend this imposter find this same one verse in the Bible they all lean on in common which was not stated by Paul himself, and that is 2 Peter 3:15, and when that was presented to me for the first time I almost laughed, but withheld the urge out of courtesy. What was so funny? This is the one place they find what they believe to be any support at all, and yet it appears to me to be still another proof to the contrary. Let's look at this supposed "endorsement" coming from a TRUE Apostle Peter: *"And account that the longsuffering of our Lord is salvation; even as our <u>beloved brother</u> Paul also according to the wisdom given unto him hath written unto you;"* What one word do you notice is missing from that scripture said to be an endorsement for the authority of this would-be apostle Paul? RIGHT! Peter has seemingly gone out of his way to NOT refer to Paul as an apostle! And what did he say instead? Beloved brother was the annointed title here. How many of you have ever gone to a church wedding? You go in and find a seat. Soon things begin to happen as people march in pitching flowers, etc., and before long the designated Minister steps up and begins to speak. Do you know those famous first two words which are followed by "we are gathered here"? CORRECTAMUNDO! "Dearly beloved" has been the opening line of millions of weddings, yet I am quite sure there were a few who were in attendance that would not quite qualify as apostles.

The internet is crammed with accolades for Saul, even to the extreme. It is well established that he was born in the year 5 A. D., yet you will see articles online today that declare "St. Paul the Apostle was born about the same time as Christ" *(https://kidadl.com/facts/unknown-*

apostle-paul-facts-everyone-should-know). Others will say he was only a few years younger than Christ. WHAT? The fact is, Christ lived on this earth as God in the flesh until the Resurrection when He returned to Heaven. Five years later Saul of Tarsus was born. That is 38 YEARS after the BIRTH of Jesus Christ, and 5 years after His Resurrection. What part of 5 A. D. (after death) do they not understand?

But before we go any further into the life of Saul, it will be important to note the very harsh exchanges between Jesus Christ and Saul's bretheren the Jews. In John 8:22 the Jews, and it does read Jews very plainly, said unto Him, Who art thou? As Christ was beginning to explain things we find later in verse 31 that Christ replied to "those Jews which believed on Him". This is worthy of note because they are claiming to be His followers, but Christ was not fooled, He knew better, and for good reason as we will learn a bit later. But right here in the conversation they were having, it is my view that Christ sprung a BRILLIANT trap for these Jews, and they took the bait, as they say... "hook, line and sinker". Christ said, ***"If ye continue in my word, then are ye my disciples indeed; And ye shall know the truth, and the truth shall make you free".*** This is a very well known and quoted piece of scripture, but not so many realize the HUGE significance of the answer in reply from the Jews; *"We be of Abraham's seed, and were never in bondage to any man: how sayest thou, Ye shall be made free?"* At this point Christ was clever to not reveal what He just made these imposters admit; that if they were never in bondage to any man, then they have just admitted of themselves to be NO PART of the 12 Tribes of Israel coming out of Egypt led by Moses, or the Babylonian captivity either, yet they will continue to pretend FALSELY that they are Israelites of the 12 Tribes. But this falsehood is exposed even in their own Jewish Almanac of 1980, p.3 where it reads: *"Strictly speaking, it is incorrect to call an ancient Israelite a 'Jew', or to call a contemporary Jew and Israelite or a Hebrew."* Also confirmed in the Encyclopedia Judaica

1971, Vol. 10:23, where it reads: *"Edomite Jews began to call themselves Hebrews and Israelites in 1860."* And there you have it straight from... well, there you have it! The Jews confess.

These Edomite Jews as well as the Khazarian Jews have come from the far east originally, and going back in their ancestry to the start you will find they are the sons of CAIN. How do we know this? Because we trust in the words of Jesus Christ. We look now to Matthew 23, where Christ spends most of the chapter telling the Jews how horrible they are, repeatedly saying throughout several verses, ***"WOE UNTO YOU, SCRIBES AND PHARISEES, HYPOCRITES!"*** Also calling them a generation *(as in a family, or descendency)* OF VIPERS, ***"HOW CAN YOU ESCAPE THE DAMNATION OF HELL?***

But the proof I mentioned earlier about how Christ reveals to us that these Jews have descended from Cain is found in Matt. 23:35, where He says, ***"That upon you may come all the righteous blood shed upon the earth, from the blood of <u>righteous Abel</u> unto the blood of Zacharias son of Barachias, whom ye slew between the temple and the altar."*** Christ just told you in this very revealing Bible verse that the ANCESTRY of these Jews standing in front of Him killed righteous Abel! It also just so happens that this particular passage is still another proof that unless this ancestry of Jews were very good swimmers, Noah's Flood was definitely NOT worldwide, or they could not have done what Christ said they did without interruption throughout all that time going back to the beginning right through the flood era.

We also learn from this verse that while Christ KNOWS that Cain was the son of Satan, He also knows and reveals that Abel was NOT. We know this because there is no way Christ would refer to any son of Satan as RIGHTEOUS. Therfore, the action described in Gen 4:1

is what produced "Righteous" Abel, while the original pregnancy was consumated in Gen. 3 between Satan and Eve. But getting back to our pursuit of Saul's/Paul's Jewish ancestry, the much BIGGER NEWS is yet to come! Let's flip back over to John 8:44-47, where Christ confirms to us that Cain's father was SATAN, and that those Jews standing in front of Him would never understand Him because they were not of God, but instead were of their father Satan!

"Ye are of your father the devil, and the lusts of your father ye will do. He was a murderer from the beginning, and abode not in the truth, because there is no truth in him. When he speaketh a lie, he speaketh of his own: for he is a liar, and the father of it. And because I tell you the truth, ye believe me not. Which of you convinceth me of sin? And if I say the truth, why do ye not believe me? He that is of God heareth God's words: ye therefore hear them not, because ye are not of God."

And why did I say that Christ CONFIRMED that Cain's father was Satan? Let's turn now to Genesis 3: verses 13 and 15 and see what the Heavenly Father told us about this in the beginning. In verse 13, Eve is confessing to God, and despite what we have been led to believe in our Bible all of our lives, the harsh reality is that in the Hebrew language (which thankfully has NEVER changed) we get the REAL truth about "the original sin". And it has NOTHING to do with Eve eating an apple offered to her by a talking snake. In the Hebrew, Eve says the nacash (naw-khash') meaning enchanter or magician... nasha' (naw-shaw') me, meaning seduced me utterly... and I did eat (in Hebrew meaning either to consume food, to do with, or to LAY with sexually). So, the enchanter (Satan) seduced Eve and they did have sex. Now it is established that Eve will bring forth Satan's child, and God declared to Satan, *"And I will put enmity between thee* (Satan)

9

and the woman, and between thy seed (Cain) and her seed (with Adam of her own race; Abel, Seth and siblings); *it shall bruise thy head, and thou shalt bruise his heel."* The word seed appears in the KJV Bible 254 times. Forty times it is a reference to a plant or vegetation starter, and 214 times it means progeny, or child such as Abraham's seed, etc.

So now to close the loop, how can we be sure that this "enchanter or magician" was actually Satan? Once again we will trust the words of Christ from several sources. First, the previously mentioned John 8:44, as He said to the Jews... ***"Ye are of your father the DEVIL..."***. Then, we look to John 6:70,71 as Christ would choose a Satanic JEW (descendant of Cain) to BE SURE to get a betrayal and therefore carry out His Divine Mission to go to the Cross and lay down His life for HIS PEOPLE. Christ said... ***"Have not I chosen you twelve, and one of you is a devil?*** *He spake of Judas Iscariot the son of Simon: for he it was that should betray him, being one of the twelve.* This Simon who is mentioned as the father of Judas can not be Simon Peter because Christ said that only 1 of the 12 Apostles was designated as being from the devil's race, so Judas' father could not also be an Apostle or that would mean that 2 apostles were from the devil.

And then another proof that the enchanter was Satan, also stated by Christ, is found in His EXPLANATION of the Parable of the Tares from Matt.13:36-42... *Then Jesus sent the multitude away, and went into the house: and his disciples came unto him, saying, Declare unto us the parable of the tares of the field. He answered and said unto them,* ***"He that soweth the good seed is the Son of man; The field is the world; the good seed are the children of the kingdom; but the tares are the children of the wicked one; The enemy that sowed them is the devil; the harvest is the end of the world; and the reapers are the angels. As therefore the tares are***

10

gathered and burned in the fire; so shall it be in the end of this world. The Son of man shall send forth his angels, and they shall gather out of His kingdom all things that offend, and them which do iniquity; And shall cast them into a furnace of fire: there shall be wailing and gnashing of teeth."

We also have a positive proof from another source in 1 John 3:11,12 where we read... *"For this is the message that ye heard from the beginning, that we should love one another. Not as Cain, who was of that wicked one, and slew his brother. And wherefore slew he him? Because his own works were evil, and his brother's righteous."* In the original GREEK you will find "who was THE CHILD of that wicked one" and the translators removed the mention of the child. That makes no difference. It is the same meaning either way. Strangely enough, translators removed "the child" in this passage to leave the verse reading *"...who was of".* and yet in the 3rd Chapter of Luke, in a LONG list of this same kind of ancestry reporting, the translators ADDED "the son" to each and every step of that ancestry of Mary going back to Adam! Why add it to such a multiple listing and then subtract it from just one? You know the reasom why. "They" (by now you recognize "they" as being the Jewish translators) are again hiding the matters of RACE, and in this particular case of 1 John 3:12 these evil translators are attempting to shade the truth of Cain's SATANIC race origin! A race that Christ tells us in Matthew 23 develops into world Jewry! Those who spilled ALL the righteous blood shed upon the earth from the Garden of Eden until the time of Christ AT LEAST! That is, unless you doubt the words of Jesus Christ.

And when you learn in your world history of the Bolshevik revolution where Jews murdered more than 66 MILLION Christians in the years between 1917 and 1957, and then add the World Wars, and other events which find the descendants of these Jews murdering MILLIONS of Christians, there is no doubt that the enmity placed there by God in the beginning is still in effect even today with their vaccines killing and sterilizing many millions more, (some of them selectively by vaccine batch!) while I am busy sending out this alarm in 2023! And btw, for the record, I am not suicidal.

So now it is totally clear that the self admitted Jew and Pharisee Saul of Tarsus comes by his murderous nature honest. All of his violent activity is very easy to understand knowing his ancestry. But now we ask the question, CAN A LEOPARD CHANGE HIS SPOTS? And we certainly know that can not happen naturally, but now we are down to the big question about Paul's story concerning the road to Damascus. There is no doubt in anyone's mind that God can do ANYTHING he wants to do, the question is, does GOD WANT to do anything for this descendant of Satan? That was never a factor for any of us to consider in years past when we all so eagerly believed the fairy tale of the road to Damascus, but now we consider this in an entirely different light, with more and more info coming out all the time about our history, both recently and from long ago.

Believe it or not, there are many people who are still unaware that we Americans were victims of propaganda with the details we have been made to believe about "the holocaust" as well as what truly happened in Germany with Adolf Hitler. The numbers are extremely lopsided when you compare how many millions of Christians have been murdered by these Satanic Jews vs. how many Jews (even if the 6 million death count of Jews in Germany had somehow been correct) were killed by Christians. That is because as a rule, Christians are not violent and murderous by their nature (born of the Spirit), but the Jews (born of the flesh) always have been... as Christ told us, and as accurate history reveals.

The Bible standard has always been to prove facts by 2 or more witnesses. Many will say that is why Cain did not get the punishment that he truly deserved for his murder of Abel. But as for the case of the "road to Damascus" tale, **Paul has ZERO witnesses for this event.** Furthermore, he tells this tale 3 different times in the Book of Acts, and can not keep his lies straight. First, Paul says in Acts 9:7 that *"the men which journeyed with him stood speechless, HEARING A VOICE, but seeing no man".* But then in Acts 22:9 Paul says *"they that were with him HEARD NOT THE VOICE of him that spake to me".* ALSO... Acts 26:14 *"And WE WERE ALL FALLEN to the earth"...* but Acts 9:7 reads to the contrary *"And the men which journeyed with him STOOD SPEECHLESS"...* the LIES keep piling up, and now... MORE CHANGING... Acts 9:10... the tale of a part played by "a certain disciple at Damascus named Ananias", who should go into the street that is called Straight, and enquire in the house of Judas for one called Saul of Tarsus", the tale goes on to describe how that Ananias, putting his hand on Saul, would restore his sight. THIS LIE is told in RED LETTERS as if to have been spoken by Jesus Christ himself, and how quickly it is proven a lie in Acts 26:16... once again, the RED LETTERS to signify words of CHRIST which NOW will prove one account or the other is a RED LETTER LIE! *"But rise, and stand upon thy feet: for I have appeared unto thee for this purpose, to make thee a minister and a witness both of these things which thou hast seen, and of those things in the which I will appear unto thee;"* On the one account, CHRIST did this Himself, on the other, He sent Aninias? This level of lying is completely out of control. We don't need Sherlock Holmes to figure this one out. And as we get further on into these scriptures the pattern of lying continues...

LET'S LOOK AT ACTS 26:19-20... *"Whereupon, O king Agrippa, I was not disobedient unto the heavenly vision: But shewed first unto them of Damascus, and at Jerusalem, and throughout all the coasts* of Judaea, and then to the Gentiles, that they should repent and turn to God, and do works meet for repentance." ...AND THEN COMPARE with GALATIONS 1:15-20... *"But when it pleased God, who separated me from my mother's womb, and called me by his grace, To reveal his Son in me, that I might preach him among the heathen; immediately I conferred not with flesh and blood: Neither went I up to Jerusalem to them which were apostles before me; but I went into Arabia, and returned again unto Damascus. Then after three years I went up to Jerusalem to see Peter, and abode with him fifteen days. But other of the apostles saw I none, save James the Lord's brother. Now the things which I write unto you, behold, before God, I lie not."* SO WHICH IS IT? "shewed first unto them of Damascus, and at Jerusalem, and throughout all the coasts of Judaea..." OR... the opposite and conflicting account in Galatians 1:15-20? AND WHY NOW should we believe this liar when he claims in 2 Corinthians 24 and 25... *"Of the Jews five times received I forty stripes save one. Thrice was I beaten with rods, once was I stoned, thrice I suffered shipwreck, a night and a day I have been in the deep;"* CONTRAST THIS REPORT with other times when Paul would spare himself of any mishandling by the Romans or Jews by reporting of himself to actually BE A ROMAN... so why did he not ALSO report that to avoid issues listed in 2 Corinthians 24-25? This is truly laughable when you have it all laid out in front of you.

Also, this Imposter Paul was supposedly "sent" by Jerusalem Jews to arrest and retrieve Christians from the city of Damascus which is under ROMAN RULE. What authority would Jerusalem officials have over ROMAN territories? Absolutely NONE.

PAUL declares in Romans 1:16... *"For I am not ashamed of the gospel of Christ: for it is the power of God unto salvation to every one that believeth; to the Jew first, and also to the Greek."* This lie has NEVER been the gospel of Christ either before OR AFTER the

14

resurrection... CHRIST <u>reconfirms</u> His determination that the Apostles go only to the lost sheep of the House of Israel even after the death of Judas, when showing His Hands and His Side and speaking to the 11 remaining Apostles in JOHN 20:21, saying: ***"Peace be unto you: as my Father hath sent me, even so send I you."*** No change to any "universal" gospel to "everyone". You can see many articles on the internet, all pro-Paul, which declare him the most important man in Christianity other than Christ Himself. That, of course is more NEW WORLD ORDER promotion and is there to keep alive the masquerade performed by Paul who certainly was HANDS DOWN the most influential IMPOSTER in the Gospel of Christ of all time.

And speaking of corrupting the Gospel of Christ, here is an Early American Testament to the damage done by Paul from none other than THOMAS JEFFERSON, who stated in a letter to W. Short published in The Great Thoughts by George Seldes (Ballantine Books, New York, 1985, p. 208)... *"Paul was the great Coryphaeus, and the FIRST CORRUPTOR of the doctrines of Jesus."* Coryphaeus being the leader of a party or a school of thought. Thomas Jefferson was a brilliant man and was a couple of centuries CLOSER to that time of Christ than are we in the times we currently experience. No doubt he still had access to some older books and reference materials than we have at our disposal today.

The same "scribes and Pharisees" bloodlines are bringing us our TV "FAKE NEWS" of today that have taken liberties to alter the scriptures over the years going all the way back to the time of Christ and even before. Even the young Prophet Jeremiah revealed to us in his day (before the time of Christ) that the scribes were changing the Bible texts to their own liking way back then. See Jeremiah 8:8 in Bible versions from Rotterham, Smith & Goodspeed, Moffit, Young's Literal Translation and even the Septuigent where the correct original text shows that Jeremiah said...

"How can you say we are wise, and the law of Yahweh is with us, when lo, the lying pen of the scribes has turned it into a lie." This, of course, was way too hot for the translators of the King James Version to handle, since they had so much sabotage to hide already, without admitting this so openly, so they REALLY made a mess of this verse... *"How do ye say, We are wise, and the law of the Lord is with us? Lo, certainly in vain made he it, the pen of the scribes is in vain."* WHAT? The Lord made the law in vain? And therefore the pen of the poor old scibes is also in vain? Ridiculous!

Now we will cover the why. Why would anyone want to mistranslate the Bible? The quick and easy answer is; it's the people who felt left out of the Bible before they started their sabotage. The people who God said would remain vagabonds and wanderers upon the earth without a nation of their own. Most of them today live upon a stolen piece of land in the middle east they have called Israel to hopefully benefit from confusion. Many of them live in the United States where they will not swear allegiance to the U. S. unless they can get DUAL CITIZENSHIP status. These people want to eventually rule the world with the benefit of OUR Bible changed to THEIR liking. There have been secret orders of evil men getting their power from organizing governments and laws to suit themselves throughout our history. The ORIGINAL Holy Bible in Hebrew and Greek/Aramaic is God's covenant and love letter to His people Israel (12 Tribes, Israelites) and has never been intended for anyone else, ever. When Satan sired Cain and then Cain sired the Jews, that began a bloodline of people on earth who are no part of the Bible and it's message, and who are attempting to rewrite the scriptures so that they can not only be included, but at some point, deceive even the very elect if that were possible, and rule the entire world for themselves. After the Sanhedrin officials serving the Jews had finally convinced the Romans (against their better judgement) to crucify Christ, yelling

16

"CRUCIFY HIM... CRUCIFY HIM... they immediately started their big plans to overcome the popularity of Christ and dominate the world with a church of their own.

The first major effort to start in that direction was the ministry of "THE APOSTLE PAUL". Don't you find it strange that while all the other TRUE Apostles of Christ were alive, there was no constant effort to call them selves Apostles, but it seems every time you say the name Paul, it has to be THE APOSTLE PAUL... as if to try to secure belief among the people that he indeed was an authorized Apostle, which of course, was not the case. The plan was for Paul to subvert the Gospel of Christ and create an all new Gospel which would include EVERYONE in the world. A plan to convince God's People that they are no longer expected to observe God's Law, and to preach that God's Law was pinned to the Cross and was made of none effect by the shed blood of Jesus Christ. Also preaching that everyone is born into sin and are all evil until they can come of age and "BE BORN AGAIN", a doctrine of heresy created by mistranslation and by Paul's Judeo doctrine.

None of the 7 churches to whom Paul sent his writings in Asia Minor would accept any of Paul's doctrine and they all soundly rejected those Judeo teachings completely. It was only after Paul had died and others began to try to carry on this effort did it finally get any acceptance anywhere, and that during the 2nd century A. D. This well organized movement to promote the books written by Paul finally did work their way into the "canon" of the Bible of that time. In around the third century A. D., the Catholic Church saw its beginnings evolving around Rome, and the infiltration by these Jews began almost immediately working toward the control of a world church headed by the Vatican. Many will try to fit the Vatican into the role of the antiChrist, but the reality is, the Jewish infiltrators who have no allegiance to our God, but serve their father the devil have been that spirit of anitiChrist ever since the birth of Cain, so it is not only the Jewish infiltrators in the Catholic Church, but also those Satanic Jews everywhere who are still at enmity with all of the Adamic race and will remain that way until Christ returns and completes his work as described in the parable of the Tares.

The Imposter Paul, this "most subtle beast of the Bible" can also tell some half truths and then in other places misquote verses he cites and spins to his liking from other books in the Bible. One of the most important misquotes to mention is his deletion of a very important part of Psalms 53 when he states in Romans 3:10-12... *"As it is written, There is none righteous, no, not one: There is none that understandeth, there is none that seeketh after God. They are all gone out of the way, they are together become unprofitable; there is none that doeth good, no, not one."* That is a very bleak picture he painted of the entire population, and it is a deliberate and purposeful sabotage attempting to make children of the Kingdom of God think that they are born a sinful creation with the most evil nature possible just like Paul, and must commit to certain prescribed works before they die to "GET SAVED" or they will go to Hell. Where did he get this damnable heresy? It is his nature, because he is a Jew, born spritually dead from the womb, and he thinks everybody is that way, or actually, wants to convince you that you are just like him. So how did he misquote? In the 53rd Psalm from which he was quoting, he purposefully eliminated the beginning part of the message which states; *"THE FOOL HATH SAID IN HIS HEART, THERE IS NO GOD* (and then continuing) *Corrupt are they* (fools), *and have done abominable iniquity: there is none* (fools) *that doeth good. God looked down from heaven upon the children of men, to see if there were any* (fools) *that did understand, that did seek God. Every one of them* (fools) *is gone back: they* (fools) *are altogether become filthy; there is none* (fools) *that doeth good, no, not one. Have the workers of iniquity* (fools) *no knowledge? who eat up MY PEOPLE* (NOT FOOLS) *as they eat bread: they (fools) have not called upon God."* What a demonic spin Paul has placed upon this entire thought. These workers of iniquity who eat up GOD'S PEOPLE like they eat bread are the fools that doeth no good, not God's people! And from this heresy comes the doctrine that all are born in sin when the truth of the matter is, CHRIST told us the exact opposite of that. He said in John 3:3 ***"...Except a man be born ANOTHEN, he cannot see the kingdom of God."*** Surprised? Do you think that is incorrect? Go ahead and check Strong's concordance to find the GREEK term there which the translators replaced with the word AGAIN, and you will find that it had originally been ANOTHEN. And what does "anothen" mean? It means FROM ABOVE! Christ actually said you must be born FROM ABOVE to see the Kingdom of God. And then after the ridiculous translator additive verse 4 with Nicodemus saying, *"can he enter the second time into his mother's womb, and be born?"* (This done in an effort to help verify their mistranslation, "born again") Christ comes right back in verse 5 with clarity, and He reaffirms what He actually said in verse 3...

"Except a man be born of water (water broke) ***and of the Spirit, he cannot see the kingdom of God."*** Note that the word Spirit here is Capital "S" to signify the presence of Deity, as in "Born of the Spirit OF GOD", not just born in a good mood. The Jew Nicodemus came right back and asked, "How can these things be?" Christ knew that he would never understand because he, being a Jewish descendant of Cain was born spiritually dead from the womb, WITHOUT the Spirit of God, just like Paul and the rest of this Satanic bloodline. NOW verse 6 will make really good sense to many of you for possibly the very first time... ***"That which is born of the flesh*** (WITHOUT the Spirit of God) ***is flesh, and that which is born of the Spirit*** (SPIRIT OF GOD) ***is Spirit."*** SO... marvel not that Christ said, Ye must be born FROM ABOVE! Our God chooses us, not the other way around as

Paul and the translators are trying to assert with their born "AGAIN" mistranslation!

And even more confusion was spun by Paul as he attempted to change God's determination ordained in the covenant which God made for His covenant people Israel. These descendants of Jacob were God's people through birthright, and had NOTHING to do with faith, even though God's people are born with faith and with His laws written in their hearts FROM BIRTH. Here is how that is distorted by The Imposter Paul in Romans 4:13... *"For the promise, that he should be the heir of the world, was not to Abraham, or to his seed, through the law, but through the righteousness of faith."* This is pure and utter nonsense.

Here is another of many places where the Imposter Paul tries to create his new gospel-in-disguise with subtle comments which are contrary to the words of Christ... Romans 1:11... "For I long to see you, that I may impart unto you some spiritual gift, to the end ye may be established..." Here we see two damages to the Gospel of Christ, first the very idea that PAUL himself will be the deliverer of a spritual gift, and also the idea that this gift was NOT embedded at birth as is stated in the Gospel of Christ... ye must be BORN FROM ABOVE. Paul's terminology stating and hoping that ye MAY BE established (at some point in the future) is heresy. This is still another variation and difference between Paul and Jesus Christ. It is a play off the mistranslation BORN AGAIN. According to Christ, it matters that you are born with the Spirit of God, or you will never see the Kingdom of Heaven (John 3:5). Christ also told us in an important passage found on Mark 4:10-12 that there are some on this earth who are born WITHOUT the Spirit of God... *And when he was alone, they that were about him with the twelve asked of him the parable. And he said unto them,* ***"Unto you it is given to know the mystery of the king-dom of God: but unto them that are without, all these*** *things are done in parables: That seeing they may see, and not perceive; and hearing they may hear, and not understand; lest at any time they should be converted, and their sins should be forgiven them."* WOW! Ask your Pastor about that one, huh? Christ said those who are born WITHOUT (the Spirit of God) should only hear parables which they will not understand because if they did understand they should be converted and He would be forced to forgive their sins. THIS tells you just exactly how far today's churches have gone of the rails!

Another verse from the second chapter of Romans in verse 11 (again) declares emphatically... "For there is no respect of persons with God." This is only true of individuals within a particular race of people. When looking at this UNIVERSALLY, God most definitely will divide HIS sheep from THE goats. In that respect, he will most definitely be a respector of persons, but again Paul is setting up a vague term to be misunderstood by millons over the centuries. Here is what Christ revealed about God's respect of persons in terms of NATIONS or RACES of people as shown in Matthew 25:31-34... *"When the Son of man shall come in his glory, and all the holy angels with him, then shall he sit upon the throne of his glory: And before him shall be gathered all NATIONS: and he shall separate them one from another, as a shepherd divideth his sheep from the goats: And he shall set the sheep on his right hand, but the goats on the left. Then shall the King say unto them on his right hand, Come, ye blessed of my Father, inherit the kingdom prepared for you from the foundation of the world:"* This is definitely a statement made about dividing the people into groups rathers than by individuals, and the end determination by God is done by GROUP, not individuals also. But you can see the deceitful way that Paul is attempting to change that with the idea that each individual will be considered on his own merits, with NO regard to the Covenant of God and HIS people Israel. Subtle is not a term that is harsh enough to describe this sort of heresy, but subtle is a reminder of the father of Paul's Satanic race of people... "the most subtle beast of the field" (Gen. 3:1).

Looking into Galatians 1:9 we see Paul setting up a basis for chastising you if you do not believe his Judaized Gospel: *"As we said before, so say I now again, If any man preach any other gospel unto you than that ye have received, let him be accursed."* Sound familiar? Does that sound to you anything like today's totally bogus charge of anti-semitism which is constantly being alleged by Paul's modern day Jewish bretheren? This disgusting word rears it's ugly head every time something is said with which the Jews do not agree! "If we don't like what you say, you're in trouble!" This seems to always be a very distinct pattern of the Jews for sure.

And now we should look at one of the most confusing statements of all the twisted texts coming from one who claims to be an Apostle of Jesus Christ, Acts 26:9... *"I verily thought with myself, that I ought to do many things contrary to the name of Jesus of Nazareth."* OK, go ahead and say it. I know what comes next... YOU THINK I AM TAKING THAT OUT OF CONTEXT! That is always the response when there is no logical argument to support a view, idea or a way of thinking. Well this statement is NOT taken out of context whatsoever, it is just quite simply a very, very strange comment indeed. And while on the topic of strange comments, take note of Paul's suggestion that he may be something more than just a mortal man when he adds a statement at the end of Romans 3:5 to remind us that in this particular verse, he is speaking to us as a man. The only reason for that to be there is to assert that there are other times when he is NOT speaking as a man. This is classic narcissism on display for all to see.

What more damage can Paul possibly do to the legacy of Jesus Christ? We know Christ was God in the flesh. Christ told us plainly in John 10:30... *"I and my Father are one."* So what does Paul do about all that? He makes a HUGE effort to destroy the idea that Christ was God in the flesh. I have a file of over 120 verses from the writings which are attributed to Paul (and those influenced by him) that go out of their way to attempt to separate Christ from The Father, seemingly at every possible turn... (listed at the end of this book).

And now that I have pointed that out to you, you're going to see it constantly in all of Paul's writings, everywhere you look! Paul seems to be attempting to create the notion that Christ and His Father are TWO... constantly! The fact is they are BOTH ONE AND TWO, but not always separate as TWO the way Paul wants to assert. It just seems that once you start to notice these things, you will find them everywhere you turn, Paul is the OPPOSITE of Christ, in every possible way. And when you do know of the origin of Paul's Satanic race it begins to make perfect sense. Paul is in tune with HIS father, the devil.

Now with Paul coming of age at around 25 to 30 A. D. and then dying at 65 A. D., his time as a false prophet and a liar is documented with perfect timing by Christ in His message to John on the Isle of Patmos in 96 A. D., only about 30 years later. Revelation 2:2 is surely an acknowledgement of The Imposter Paul in a message that Christ told John to write unto the church at Ephesus. Christ says: *"I know thy works, and thy labour, and thy patience, and how thou canst not bear them which are evil: and thou hast tried them which say they are apostles, and are not, and hast found them liars..."* It is also in this 2nd chapter of Revelation in verse 9 that we get still another confirmation about the origin of the Jews as told by Christ: *"I know thy works, and tribulation, and poverty, (but thou art rich) and I know the blasphemy of them which say they are Jews* (in the

23

sense of a country, Israelite Judeaens), **and are not, but are the synagogue of Satan."** Well, I don't know what you think as we go through these Biblical facts one by one, but one thing is for certain, we ALL can easily detect what Christ thinks about these Jews, aka the scribes and Pharisees... without a doubt. I will always believe what Christ says, and I will leave your beliefs up to you.

In John 5:18 we find the Jews were ready to kill Christ and then later in verses 42-43, Christ makes a prophecy which no doubt came true when Paul began to preach a strange "gospel". Paul's gospel suited the Jews much better than the "narrow nationalisms" and the "endless geneologies" which were always important to God, but were always scorned by Paul. In that passage Christ said to the Jews...
"But I know you, that ye have not the love of God in you. I am come in my Father's name, and ye receive me not: if another shall come in his own name, him ye will receive." Just 5 years after the resurrection Christ was back in heaven and Paul was born. His preaching later birthed a new doctrine totally contrary to that of Jesus Christ, and the Jews did receive him just as Christ had said in His prophecy from John 5:42-43.

So it all comes down to THE BIG LIE. Are you by now wondering which of ALL of the lies that would be? No, of course not. The entire premise of the validity of Paul as an Apostle depends upon your belief in the BIGGEST of all of his lies.. that fairy tale of his unwitnessed "conversion" on the road to Damascus. And it is pretty plain that Paul would seem to be confessing of this obvious lie when you read one of the most astonishing questions in the entire Bible as it was posed by Paul in ROMANS 3:7... *"For if the truth of God hath more abounded through my lie unto his glory; why yet am I also judged as a sinner?"* What is the most important feature to notice in this question? That's right, Paul is asking about a LIE in the SINGULAR, not plural (lies), and he certainly seems to be admitting that his "conversion" story is a lie by asking if it is really that important as long as God gets the glory from his lie... SICK! My immediate response is probably the same as yours, what kind of person would think God needs glory that was gained by a LIE, right? (A Satanic Jew, that's who!) Do you believe "his lie", or are you starting to have your doubts about this fairy tale of the road to Damascus?

Most will admit, the picture is altogether different when you get the true translations of some key terms in the story of Eve, and the reality of the Satanic bloodline that spawned the Jewish race. I, for one, will not call Christ a liar. If you are also a believer in Jesus Christ, and trust His word, then surely you feel the same way. Do yourself a HUGE favor. Verify these things I am telling you with YOUR OWN research into these scriptures I have given you revealing the words from Christ. Read more than just the verses shown, and instead read the entire chapters for full and complete context. In fact, you should MOST ESPECIALLY READ MATTHEW 23 and also JOHN 8 both in FULL! Also do not rely upon the verification of others, ESPECIALLY the Pastors or Ministers who will be feeling challenged to defend the things they may have been preaching to the contrary, especially with regard to things they may have been taught in the various Judaic Semenaries that corrupted America in the 1930's, 40's and ever since with the Satanic doctrines of the Jewish Imposter Paul. Also, please DO NOT BLAME the Pastors for their inability to foresee the troubles these false doctrines have caused many millions of believers, especially in the past 6 or 7 decades. The Bible tells us that knowledge would increase and things would be understood differently in the scriptures as a result. Certainly that has become evident to all of us in recent years. Nobody could have known in advance the kind of knowledge and awareness that would flourish due to the advent of the information highway we now refer to as the internet.

I stand with our Pastors who have defended the Word of God through thick and thin, especially against the many incroachments by the Government. In fact we all, myself included, must forgive ourselves for not recognizing these things before now, and be willing to accept truth when we finally do see it. Because after you have seen it... you can't UNSEE IT! You will wonder as I do right now how I EVER missed all these things for my entire life while claiming to be a fairly regular Bible reader. It is like Mark Twain once said... *"It is easier to fool someone, than to convince them they HAVE BEEN FOOLED"*. And you know that is right, for sure. The truth from Jesus Christ is impossible to refute in my opinion. So we need to heal over this and move on, even though it seems to be a very, very hard thing to do. Our nations need to heal... and it feels like our very souls need to heal and get past the most dark period of this age that we could possibly have imagined.

We have innocently, but incorrectly believed with blind faith that our Bibles were protected from sabotage, just as we had every right to believe our television news was always truthful. But "FAKE NEWS" did not just begin when President Trump began to call out the television networks for not only "shading" the news, or simply presenting it with a slant, but outright LYING. Former Director of the CIA William Casey said back in 1981... *"We'll know our disinformation program is complete when EVERYTHING the American public believes is false."* It has been 42 years since then. They are caught in lie after lie, yet amazingly they are still believed by some very lazy listeners.

And while on the topic of our government, for those who did not know, a law was passed in this nation years ago to allow our government to use propaganda abroad in any country other than our own, for whatever purpose or reason they deemed necessary under the guise of our "national security". Even fewer of us know that more recently, barry obama signed into law the change that made possible the same use of propaganda by our own government against WE THE PEOPLE as well as against the rest of the world! So we actually do have every right to question our corrupt government, and their partners in crime in the "mainstream media" about anything and everything, and the same goes for those modern day scribes and Pharisees who are STILL perverting the Holy Bible, century after century, and more recently, version after version.

The clinching piece of this whole question of Paul's authority as an apostle of Jesus Christ, and of the Jewish control and eventual world domination of the entire planet is not answered by any one lie or however many lies were told by The Imposter Paul, but instead is a very bold, authoritative and decisive statement made by Jesus Christ. If you are still "sitting on the fence" on this matter, get ready to be blown off. In Acts 23:6, Paul openly admitted in a council meeting of the Jewish Sanhedrin that he was a Pharisee and his father was a Pharisee as well. That is about to become astonishingly important in this story of The Imposter Paul, because Christ said in Matt. 5:20... ***"For I say unto you, That except your righteousness shall exceed the righteousness of the scribes and Pharisees, ye shall in no case enter into the kingdom of heaven."*** There is NO WAY to get around this one. Christ knew and actually told us that this Satanic bloodline of Jews, scribes and Pharisees sprang up from the Garden of Eden and has been at enmity with Adam's race ever since. And if this Pharisee Paul and all of his brethren shall in NO CASE enter into the kingdom of Heaven, then we also know that he could in NO CASE ever, ever have been an Apostle of Jesus Christ! AMEN.

PROLOGUE

Connecting the dots from the words of Jesus Christ was the only way to write this book. So I can not take credit for writing the facts offered, just possibly an attaboy for assembling the Holy Bread Crumbs left behind by our Lord and Savior Jesus Christ. So after reading this assembly, if you disgree with the premise offered by Christ concerning the origin of the Jews, that is up to you. But realize that you are disagreeing with Christ, and not with me. I am just the messenger. I always have said...

ARGUE WITH CHRIST AT YOUR OWN PERIL!

CONGRATULATIONS upon graduating to the knowledge that indeed our HOLY BIBLE has been molested by our mortal enemy and his literal children upon this earth. You have learned of much of this from reading this book, and if you are thirsting for more knowledge in the area of sabotaged scriptures you should make your way to the website:

originaltruth2022.com

Get a copy of the ALL-IN-ONE version of

ORIGINAL TRUTH

or at least the condensed study version:

ORIGINAL TRUTH BIBLE COMPANION

to further your studies and even more importantly...

to support the preservation of

GOD'S HOLY WORD

The children of the kingdom of God

WRESTLE EVERY DAY

with the flesh and blood descendants
of Satan aka sons of Cain
aka Kenites aka Edomites
aka Khazarians
aka "the JEW"
who have assumed powers of principalities by deceit,
who are rulers of the darkness of this world,
representing spiritual wickedness in high places.

This is the truth that The Imposter Paul was hiding from you in
Ephesians 6:12

Mediator...

is a term found in 9 verses of the KJV of the Holy Bible. All 9 were written by the

IMPOSTER PAUL

along with OVER 120 other
verses trying in vain to show
that Christ and The Father

ARE TWO!!!

The writings of Paul are also the ONLY place where you will find the disrespectful presentation of the name of JESUS CHRIST shown BACKWARDS!

NOBODY WANTS TO BE REFERRED TO IN THAT FASHION!

In 1 Timothy 2:5 we see the worst of both COMBINED:

"For there is one God, and one mediator between God and men, the man Christ Jesus"

John 10:30... "I and my Father are ONE" — Jesus Christ

It is one way or the other... WHO DO YOU BELIEVE?

Get a fabulous "aid" for your Bible reading!

originaltruth2022.com

Offering keys for better understanding of your HOLY BIBLE!

ACT 2:22... Ye men of Israel, hear these words; Jesus of Nazareth, a man approved of God among you by miracles and wonders and signs, which God did by him in the midst of you, as ye yourselves also know:

ACT 2:36... Therefore let all the house of Israel know assuredly, that God hath made that same Jesus, whom ye have crucified, both Lord and Christ.

ACT 3:13... The God of Abraham, and of Isaac, and of Jacob, the God of our fathers, hath glorified his Son Jesus; whom ye delivered up, and denied him in the presence of Pilate, when he was determined to let him go.

ACT 3:26... Unto you first God, having raised up his Son Jesus, sent him to bless you, in turning away every one of you from his iniquities.

ACT 4:10... Be it known unto you all, and to all the people of Israel, that by the name of Jesus Christ of Nazareth, whom ye crucified, whom God raised from the dead, even by him doth this man stand here before you whole.

ACT 4:26... The kings of the earth stood up, and the rulers were gathered together against the Lord, and against his Christ.

ACT 5:30... The God of our fathers raised up Jesus, whom ye slew and hanged on a tree.

ACT 7:55... But he, being full of the Holy Ghost, looked up stedfastly into heaven, and saw the glory of God, and Jesus standing on the right hand of God,

ACT 7:56... And said, Behold, I see the heavens opened, and the Son of man standing on the right hand of God.

ACT 8:12... But when they believed Philip preaching the things concerning the kingdom of God, and the name of Jesus Christ, they were baptized, both men and women.

ACT 10:38... How God anointed Jesus of Nazareth with the Holy Ghost and with power: who went about doing good, and healing all that were oppressed of the devil; for God was with him.

ACT 20:21... Testifying both to the Jews, and also to the Greeks, repentance toward God, and faith toward our Lord Jesus Christ.

ROM 1:1... Paul, a servant of Jesus Christ, called to be an apostle, separated unto the gospel of God,

ROM 1:4... And declared to be the Son of God with power, according to the spirit of holiness, by the resurrection from the dead:

ROM 1:7... To all that be in Rome, beloved of God, called to be saints: Grace to you and peace from God our Father, and the Lord Jesus Christ.

ROM 1:8... First, I thank my God through Jesus Christ for you all, that your faith is spoken of throughout the whole world.

ROM 1:9... For God is my witness, whom I serve with my spirit in the gospel of his Son,

ROM 1:16... For I am not ashamed of the gospel of Christ: for it is the power of God unto salvation to every one that believeth; to the Jew first, and also to the Greek.

ROM 2:16... In the day when God shall judge the secrets of men by Jesus Christ according to my gospel.

ROM 5:1... Therefore being justified by faith, we have peace with God through our Lord Jesus Christ:

ROM 5:8... But God commendeth his love toward us, in that, while we were yet sinners, Christ died for us.

ROM 5:10... For if, when we were enemies, we were reconciled to God by the death of his Son, much more, being reconciled, we shall be saved by his life.

ROM 5:11... And not only so, but we also joy in God through our Lord Jesus Christ, by whom we have now received the atonement.

ROM 5:15... But not as the offence, so also is the free gift. For if through the offence of one many be dead, much more the grace of God, and the gift by grace, which is by one man, Jesus Christ, hath abounded unto many.

ROM 6:11... Likewise reckon ye also yourselves to be dead indeed unto sin, but alive unto God through Jesus Christ our Lord.

ROM 6:23... For the wages of sin is death; but the gift of God is eternal life through Jesus Christ our Lord.

ROM 7:4... Wherefore, my brethren, ye also are become dead to the law by the body of Christ; that ye should be married to another, even to him who is raised from the dead, that we should bring forth fruit unto God.

ROM 7:25... I thank God through Jesus Christ our Lord. So then with the mind I myself serve the law of God; but with the flesh the law of sin.

ROM 8:3... For what the law could not do, in that it was weak through the flesh, God sending his own Son in the likeness of sinful flesh, and for sin, condemned sin in the flesh:

ROM 8:17... And if children, then heirs; heirs of God, and joint-heirs with Christ; if so be that we suffer with him, that we may be also glorified together.

ROM 8:28,29... And we know that all things work together for good to them that love God, to them who are the called according to his purpose. For whom he did foreknow, he also did predestinate to be conformed to the image of his Son, that he might be the firstborn among many brethren.

ROM 8:31... What shall we then say to these things? If God be for us, who can be against us? He that spared not his own Son, but delivered him up for us all, how shall he not with him also freely give us all things?

ROM 8:34... Who is he that condemneth? It is Christ that died, yea rather, that is risen again, who is even at the right hand of God, who also maketh intercession for us.

ROM 15:6... That ye may with one mind and one mouth glorify God, even the Father of our Lord Jesus Christ.

ROM 15:7... Wherefore receive ye one another, as Christ also received us to the glory of God.

ROM 15:16... That I should be the minister of Jesus Christ to the Gentiles, ministering the gospel of God, that the offering up of the Gentiles might be acceptable, being sanctified by the Holy Ghost.

ROM 15:17... I have therefore whereof I may glory through Jesus Christ in those things which pertain to God.

ROM 15:19... Through mighty signs and wonders, by the power of the Spirit of God; so that from Jerusalem, and round about unto Illyricum, I have fully preached the gospel of Christ.

ROM 15:30... Now I beseech you, brethren, for the Lord Jesus Christ's sake, and for the love of the Spirit, that ye strive together with me in your prayers to God for me;

ROM 16:20... And the God of peace shall bruise Satan under your feet shortly. The grace of our Lord Jesus Christ be with you. Amen.

1 COR 1:3... Grace be unto you, and peace, from God our Father, and from the Lord Jesus Christ.

1 COR 1:4... I thank my God always on your behalf, for the grace of God which is given you by Jesus Christ;

1 COR 1:9... God is faithful, by whom ye were called unto the fellowship of his Son Jesus Christ our Lord.

1 COR 1:24... But unto them which are called, both Jews and Greeks, Christ the power of God, and the wisdom of God.

1 COR 1:30... But of him are ye in Christ Jesus, who of God is made unto us wisdom, and righteousness, and sanctification, and redemption:

1 COR 3:23... And ye are Christ's; and Christ is God's.

1 COR 4:1... Let a man so account of us, as of the ministers of Christ, and stewards of the mysteries of God.

1 COR 8:6... But to us there is but one God, the Father, of whom are all things, and we in him; and one Lord Jesus Christ, by whom are all things, and we by him.

1 COR 9:21... To them that are without law, as without law, (being not without law to God, but under the law to Christ,) that I might gain them that are without law.

1 COR 11:3... But I would have you know, that the head of every man is Christ; and the head of the woman is the man; and the head of Christ is God.

1 COR 15:15... Yea, and we are found false witnesses of God; because we have testified of God that he raised up Christ:

1 COR 15:57... But thanks be to God, which giveth us the victory through our Lord Jesus Christ.

2 COR 1:1... Paul, an apostle of Jesus Christ by the will of God, and Timothy our brother, unto the church of God which is at Corinth, with all the saints which are in all Achaia:

2 COR 1:2... Grace be to you and peace from God our Father, and from the Lord Jesus Christ.

2 COR 1:3... Blessed be God, even the Father of our Lord Jesus Christ, the Father of mercies, and the God of all comfort;

2 COR 1:19... For the Son of God, Jesus Christ, who was preached among you by us, even by me and Silvanus and Timotheus, was not yea and nay, but in him was yea.

2 COR 2:14... Now thanks be unto God, which always causeth us to triumph in Christ, and maketh manifest the savour of his knowledge by us in every place.

2 COR 2:17... For we are not as many, which corrupt the word of God: but as of sincerity, but as of God, in the sight of God speak we in Christ.

2 COR 3:4... And such trust have we through Christ to God-ward:

2 COR 4:4... In whom the god of this world hath blinded the minds of them which believe not, lest the light of the glorious gospel of Christ, who is the image of God, should shine unto them.

2 COR 4:6... For God, who commanded the light to shine out of darkness, hath shined in our hearts, to give the light of the knowledge of the glory of God in the face of Jesus Christ.

2 COR 5:18... And all things are of God, who hath reconciled us to himself by Jesus Christ, and hath given to us the ministry of reconciliation;

2 COR 5:20... Now then we are ambassadors for Christ, as though God did beseech you by us: we pray you in Christ's stead, be ye reconciled to God.

2 COR 9:13... Whiles by the experiment of this ministration they glorify God for your professed subjection unto the gospel of Christ, and for your liberal distribution unto them, and unto all men;

2 COR 10:5... Casting down imaginations, and every high thing that exalteth itself against the knowledge of God, and bringing into captivity every thought to the obedience of Christ;

2 COR 11:31... The God and Father of our Lord Jesus Christ, which is blessed for evermore, knoweth that I lie not.

2 COR 13:14... The grace of the Lord Jesus Christ, and the love of God, and the communion of the Holy Ghost, be with you all.

GAL 1:1... Paul, an apostle, (not of men, neither by man, but by Jesus Christ, and God the Father, who raised him from the dead;)

GAL 1:3... Grace be to you and peace from God the Father, and from our Lord Jesus Christ,

GAL 2:20... I am crucified with Christ: nevertheless I live; yet not I, but Christ liveth in me: and the life which I now live in the flesh I live by the faith of the Son of God, who loved me, and gave himself for me.

GAL 2:21... I do not frustrate the grace of God: for if righteousness come by the law, then Christ is dead in vain.

GAL 3:26... For ye are all the children of God by faith in Christ Jesus.

GAL 4:4... But when the fulness of the time was come, God sent forth his Son, made of a woman, made under the law,

GAL 4:6... And because ye are sons, God hath sent forth the Spirit of his Son into your hearts, crying, Abba, Father.

GAL 4:7... Wherefore thou art no more a servant, but a son; and if a son, then an heir of God through Christ.

GAL 4:14... And my temptation which was in my flesh ye despised not, nor rejected; but received me as an angel of God, even as Christ Jesus.

EPH 1:1... Paul, an apostle of Jesus Christ by the will of God, to the saints which are at Ephesus, and to the faithful in Christ Jesus:

EPH 1:2... Grace be to you, and peace, from God our Father, and from the Lord Jesus Christ.

EPH 1:3... Blessed be the God and Father of our Lord Jesus Christ, who hath blessed us with all spiritual blessings in heavenly places in Christ:

EPH 1:5... Having predestinated us unto the adoption of children by Jesus Christ to himself, according to the good pleasure of his will...

EPH 1:20... Which he wrought in Christ, when he raised him from the dead, and set him at his own right hand in the heavenly places,

EPH 2:4&5... But God, who is rich in mercy, for his great love wherewith he loved us, Even when we were dead in sins, hath quickened us together with Christ, (by grace ye are saved;)

EPH 2:10... For we are his workmanship, created in Christ Jesus unto good works, which God hath before ordained that we should walk in them.

EPH 2:12... That at that time ye were without Christ, being aliens from the commonwealth of Israel, and strangers from the covenants of promise, having no hope, and without God in the world:

EPH 3:9... And to make all men see what is the fellowship of the mystery, which from the beginning of the world hath been hid in God, who created all things by Jesus Christ:

EPH 3:14... For this cause I bow my knees unto the Father of our Lord Jesus Christ,

EPH 3:19... And to know the love of Christ, which passeth knowledge, that ye might be filled with all the fulness of God.

EPH 4:13... Till we all come in the unity of the faith, and of the knowledge of the Son of God, unto a perfect man, unto the measure of the stature of the fulness of Christ:

EPH 4:32... And be ye kind one to another, tenderhearted, forgiving one another, even as God for Christ's sake hath forgiven you.

EPH 5:5... For this ye know, that no whoremonger, nor unclean person, nor covetous man, who is an idolater, hath any inheritance in the kingdom of Christ and of God.

EPH 5:20... Giving thanks always for all things unto God and the Father in the name of our Lord Jesus Christ;

EPH 5:23... Peace be to the brethren, and love with faith, from God the Father and the Lord Jesus Christ.

PHI 1:2... Grace be unto you, and peace, from God our Father, and from the Lord Jesus Christ.

PHI 1:11... Being filled with the fruits of righteousness, which are by Jesus Christ, unto the glory and praise of God.

PHI 2:11... And that every tongue should confess that Jesus Christ is Lord, to the glory of God the Father.

PHI 2:22... But ye know the proof of him, that, as a son with the father, he hath served with me in the gospel.

PHI 3:3... For we are the circumcision, which worship God in the spirit, and rejoice in Christ Jesus, and have no confidence in the flesh.

PHI 3:14... I press toward the mark for the prize of the high calling of God in Christ Jesus.

PHI 4:7... And the peace of God, which passeth all understanding, shall keep your hearts and minds through Christ Jesus.

PHI 4:19... But my God shall supply all your need according to his riches in glory by Christ Jesus.

COL 1:1... Paul, an apostle of Jesus Christ by the will of God, and Timotheus our brother,

COL 1:2... To the saints and faithful brethren in Christ which are at Colosse: Grace be unto you, and peace, from God our Father and the Lord Jesus Christ.

COL 1:3... We give thanks to God and the Father of our Lord Jesus Christ, praying always for you,

COL 1:13... Who hath delivered us from the power of darkness, and hath translated us into the kingdom of his dear Son:

COL 1:27... To whom God would make known what is the riches of the glory of this mystery among the Gentiles; which is Christ in you, the hope of glory:

COL 3:1... If ye then be risen with Christ, seek those things which are above, where Christ sitteth on the right hand of God.

COL 3:17... And whatsoever ye do in word or deed, do all in the name of the Lord Jesus, giving thanks to God and the Father by him.

1 THE 1:1... Paul, and Silvanus, and Timotheus, unto the church of the Thessalonians which is in God the Father and in the Lord Jesus Christ: Grace be unto you, and peace, from God our Father, and the Lord Jesus Christ.

1 THE 1:3... Remembering without ceasing your work of faith, and labour of love, and patience of hope in our Lord Jesus Christ, in the sight of God and our Father;

1 THE 1:10... And to wait for his Son from heaven, whom he raised from the dead, even Jesus, which delivered us from the wrath to come.

1 THE 2:15... Who both killed the Lord Jesus, and their own prophets, and have persecuted us; and they please not God, and are contrary to all men:

1 THE 3:11... Now God himself and our Father, and our Lord Jesus Christ, direct our way unto you.

1 THE 3:13... To the end he may stablish your hearts unblameable in holiness before God, even our Father, at the coming of our Lord Jesus Christ with all his saints.

1 THE 5:9... For God hath not appointed us to wrath, but to obtain salvation by our Lord Jesus Christ,

1 THE 5:18... In every thing give thanks: for this is the will of God in Christ Jesus concerning you.

2 THE 1:1... Paul, and Silvanus, and Timotheus, unto the church of the Thessalonians in God our Father and the Lord Jesus Christ:

2 THE 1:8... In flaming fire taking vengeance on them that know not God, and that obey not the gospel of our Lord Jesus Christ:

2 THE 1:12... That the name of our Lord Jesus Christ may be glorified in you, and ye in him, according to the grace of our God and the Lord Jesus Christ.

2 THE 2:16... Now our Lord Jesus Christ himself, and God, even our Father, which hath loved us, and hath given us everlasting consolation and good hope through grace,

2 THE 3:5... And the Lord direct your hearts into the love of God, and into the patient waiting for Christ.

1 TIM 1:1... Paul, an apostle of Jesus Christ by the commandment of God our Saviour, and Lord Jesus Christ, which is our hope;

1 TIM 1:2... Unto Timothy, my own son in the faith: Grace, mercy, and peace, from God our Father and Jesus Christ our Lord.

1 TIM 2:5... For there is one God, and one mediator between God and men, the man Christ Jesus;

1 TIM 5:21... I charge thee before God, and the Lord Jesus Christ, and the elect angels, that thou observe these things without preferring one before another, doing nothing by partiality.

1 TIM 6:13... I give thee charge in the sight of God, who quickeneth all things, and before Christ Jesus, who before Pontius Pilate witnessed a good confession;

2 TIM 1:1... Paul, an apostle of Jesus Christ by the will of God, according to the promise of life which is in Christ Jesus,

2 TIM 1:2... To Timothy, my dearly beloved son: Grace, mercy, and peace, from God the Father and Christ Jesus our Lord.

2 TIM 2:19... Nevertheless the foundation of God standeth sure, having this seal, The Lord knoweth them that are his. And, Let every one that nameth the name of Christ depart from iniquity.

2 TIM 4:1... I charge thee therefore before God, and the Lord Jesus Christ, who shall judge the quick and the dead at his appearing and his kingdom;

TIT 1:1... Paul, a servant of God, and an apostle of Jesus Christ, according to the faith of God's elect, and the acknowledging of the truth which is after godliness;

TIT 1:4... To Titus, mine own son after the common faith: Grace, mercy, and peace, from God the Father and the Lord Jesus Christ our Saviour.

TIT 2:13... Looking for that blessed hope, and the glorious appearing of the great God and our Saviour Jesus Christ;

PHM 1:3... Grace to you, and peace, from God our Father and the Lord Jesus Christ.

HEB 6:1... Therefore leaving the principles of the doctrine of Christ, let us go on unto perfection; not laying again the foundation of repentance from dead works, and of faith toward God,

HEB 9:14... How much more shall the blood of Christ, who through the eternal Spirit offered himself without spot to God, purge your conscience from dead works to serve the living God?

HEB 9:24... For Christ is not entered into the holy places made with hands, which are the figures of the true; but into heaven itself, now to appear in the presence of God for us:

HEB 10:12... But this man, after he had offered one sacrifice for sins for ever, sat down on the right hand of God;

HEB 12:2...Looking unto Jesus the author and finisher of our faith; who for the joy that was set before him endured the cross, despising the shame, and is set down at the right hand of the throne of God.

And now for the examples of deceit and dihonesty from

The Imposter Paul,

here is a convenient list of SOME of the texts where he either was at odds with the words of Christ, OR where we find outright lies offered by this most subtle beast of all Bible characters other than Satan himself:

ACTS 1:8... But ye shall receive power, after that the Holy Ghost is come upon you: and ye shall be witnesses unto me both in Jerusalem, and in all Judaea, and in Samaria, and unto the uttermost part of the earth.

ACTS 8:25... returned to Jerusalem, and preached the gospel in many villages of the Samaritans.

ACTS 9:7... And the men which journeyed with him stood speechless, hearing a voice, but seeing no man.

ACTS 9:15... But the Lord said unto him, Go thy way: for he is a chosen vessel unto me, to bear my name before the Gentiles, and kings, and the children of Israel:

ACTS 9:28... And he said unto them, Ye know how that it is an unlawful thing for a man that is a Jew to keep company, or come unto one of another nation; but God hath shewed me that I should not call any man common or unclean.

45

ACTS 9:38... How God anointed Jesus of Nazareth with the Holy Ghost and with power: who went about doing good, and healing all that were oppressed of the devil; for God was with him.

ACTS 22:9... And they that were with me saw indeed the light, and were afraid; but they heard not the voice of him that spake to me.

ACTS 22:10... And I said, What shall I do, Lord? And the Lord said unto me, Arise, and go into Damascus; and there it shall be told thee of all things which are appointed for thee to do.

ACTS 22:21... And he said unto me, Depart: for I will send thee far hence unto the Gentiles.

ACTS 26:14... And when we were all fallen to the earth, I heard a voice speaking unto me, and saying in the Hebrew tongue, Saul, Saul, why persecutest thou me? it is hard for thee to kick against the pricks.

ACTS 26:16,17... But rise, and stand upon thy feet: for I have appeared unto thee for this purpose, to make thee a minister and a witness both of these things which thou hast seen, and of those things in the which I will appear unto thee; Delivering thee from the people, and from the Gentiles, unto whom now I send thee,

ACTS 26:20... But shewed first unto them of Damascus, and at Jerusalem, and throughout all the coasts of Judaea, and then to the Gentiles, that they should repent and turn to God, and do works meet for repentance.

ROMANS 1:16... For I am not ashamed of the gospel of Christ: for it is the power of God unto salvation to every one that believeth; to the Jew first, and also to the Greek.

ROMANS 3:1,2... What advantage then hath the Jew? or what profit is there of circumcision? Much every way: chiefly, because that unto them were committed the oracles of God.

ROMANS 3:7... For if the truth of God hath more abounded through my lie unto his glory; why yet am I also judged as a sinner?

ROMANS 3:10,11... As it is written, There is none righteous, no, not one: There is none that understandeth, there is none that seeketh after God.

ROMANS 3:28... Therefore we conclude that a man is justified by faith without the deeds of the law.

ROMANS 3:29... Is he the God of the Jews only? is he not also of the Gentiles? Yes, of the Gentiles also:

ROMANS 10:4... For Christ is the end of the law for righteousness to every one that believeth.

ROMANS 11:1... I say then, Hath God cast away his people? God forbid. For I also am an Israelite, of the seed of Abraham, of the tribe of Benjamin.

ROMANS 11:13,14... For I speak to you Gentiles, inasmuch as I am the apostle of the Gentiles, I magnify mine office: If by any means I may provoke to emulation them which are my flesh, and might save some of them.

ROMANS 11:27... For this is my covenant unto them, when I shall take away their sins.

1 COR. 4:15,16... For though ye have ten thousand instructors in Christ, yet have ye not many fathers: for in Christ Jesus I have begotten you through the gospel. Wherefore I beseech you, be ye followers of me.

1 COR 4:15,16... For though ye have ten thousand instructors in Christ, yet have ye not many fathers: for in Christ Jesus I have begotten you through the gospel. Wherefore I beseech you, be ye followers of me.

1 COR 7:34... There is difference also between a wife and a virgin. The unmarried woman careth for the things of the Lord, that she may be holy both in body and in spirit: but she that is married careth for the things of the world, how she may please her husband.

1 COR 12:13... For by one Spirit are we all baptized into one body, whether we be Jews or Gentiles, whether we be bond or free; and have been all made to drink into one Spirit.

1 COR 15:45... And so it is written, The first man Adam was made a living soul; the last Adam was made a quickening spirit.

2 COR 3:14... ...remaineth the same vail untaken away in the reading of the old testament; which vail is done away in Christ.

2 COR 5:15... And that he died for all, that they which live should not henceforth live unto themselves...

2 COR 5:17... Therefore if any man be in Christ, he is a new creature: old things are passed away; behold, all things are become new.

2 COR 11:8... I robbed other churches, taking wages of them, to do you service.

2 COR 11:16... Let no man think me a fool; if otherwise, yet as a fool receive me, that I may boast myself a little.

2 COR 11:24,25... Of the Jews five times received I forty stripes save one. Thrice was I beaten with rods, once was I stoned, thrice I suffered shipwreck, a night and a day I have been in the deep;

GAL 1:8,9... But though we, or an angel from heaven, preach any other gospel unto you than that which we have preached unto you, let him be accursed. As we said before, so say I now again, If any man preach any other gospel unto you than that ye have received, let him be accursed.

GAL 1:12... For I neither received it of man, neither was I taught it, but by the revelation of Jesus Christ.

GAL 1:17... Neither went I up to Jerusalem to them which were apostles before me; but I went into Arabia, and returned again unto Damascus.

GAL 1:20... Now the things which I write unto you, behold, before God, I lie not.

GAL 2:21... I do not frustrate the grace of God: for if righteousness come by the law, then Christ is dead in vain.

GAL 3:11... But that no man is justified by the law in the sight of God, it is evident: for, The just shall live by faith.

GAL 3:13... Christ hath redeemed us from the curse of the law, being made a curse for us: for it is written, Cursed is every one that hangeth on a tree:

GAL 3:16... Now to Abraham and his seed were the promises made. He saith not, And to seeds, as of many; but as of one, And to thy seed, which is Christ.

GAL 3:28,29... There is neither Jew nor Greek, there is neither bond nor free, there is neither male nor female: for ye are all one in Christ Jesus. And if ye be Christ's, then are ye Abraham's seed, and heirs according to the promise.

GAL 5:18... But if ye be led of the Spirit, ye are not under the law.

GAL 6:11... Ye see how large a letter I have written unto you with mine own hand.

EPH 5:8... For ye were sometimes darkness, but now are ye light in the Lord: walk as children of light:

EPH 6:12... For we wrestle not against flesh and blood, but against principalities...

PHI 1:7,8... ye all are partakers of my grace. For God is my record, how greatly I long after you all in the bowels of Jesus Christ.

PHI 2:6... Who, being in the form of God, thought it not robbery to be equal with God:

PHI 2:12... work out your own salvation with fear and trembling.

PHI 2:30... to supply your lack of service toward me.

PHI 3:3... and with other my fellowlabourers, whose names are in the book of life.

PHI 3:9... Those things, which ye have both learned, and received, and heard, and seen in me, do: and the God of peace shall be with you.

COL 1:23... If ye continue in the faith grounded and settled, and be not moved away from the hope of the gospel, which ye have heard, and which was preached to every creature which is under heaven; whereof I Paul am made a minister;

COL 1:27... To whom God would make known what is the riches of the glory of this mystery among the Gentiles; which is Christ in you, the hope of glory:

COL 1:28... Whom we preach, warning every man, and teaching every man in all wisdom; that we may present every man perfect in Christ Jesus:

COL 2:6... As ye have therefore received Christ Jesus the Lord, so walk ye in him:

COL 2:14... Blotting out the handwriting of ordinances that was against us, which was contrary to us, and took it out of the way, nailing it to his cross;

COL 3:11... Where there is neither Greek nor Jew, circumcision nor uncircumcision, Barbarian, Scythian, bond nor free: but Christ is all, and in all.

COL 3:14...And above all these things put on charity, which is the bond of perfectness.

1 THE 2:15... Who both killed the Lord Jesus, and their own prophets, and have persecuted us; and they please not God, and are contrary to all men:

1 THE 5:9... For God hath not appointed us to wrath, but to obtain salvation by our Lord Jesus Christ,

1 TIM 1:4... Neither give heed to fables and endless genealogies, which minister questions, rather than godly edifying which is in faith: so do.

1 TIM 1:9... Knowing this, that the law is not made for a righteous man, but for the lawless and disobedient, for the ungodly and for sinners, for unholy and profane, for murderers of fathers and murderers of mothers, for manslayers,

1 TIM 1:12... And I thank Christ Jesus our Lord, who hath enabled me, for that he counted me faithful, putting me into the ministry;

1 TIM 1:15... This is a faithful saying, and worthy of all acceptation, that Christ Jesus came into the world to save sinners; of whom I am chief.

1 TIM 2:4... Who will have all men to be saved, and to come unto the knowledge of the truth.

2 TIM 1:1... Paul, an apostle of Jesus Christ by the will of God, according to the promise of life which is in Christ Jesus,

2 TIM 1:6... Wherefore I put thee in remembrance that thou stir up the gift of God, which is in thee by the putting on of my hands.

2 TIM 3:15... And that from a child thou hast known the holy scriptures, which are able to make thee wise unto salvation through faith which is in Christ Jesus.

TIT 1:1... Paul, a servant of God, and an apostle of Jesus Christ, according to the faith of God's elect, and the acknowledging of the truth which is after godliness;

HEB 2:6... But one in a certain place testified, saying, What is man, that thou art mindful of him? or the son of man, that thou visitest him?

HEB 2:16... For verily he took not on him the nature of angels; but he took on him the seed of Abraham.

HEB 9:22... And almost all things are by the law purged with blood; and without shedding of blood is no remission.
HEB 10:12... But this man, after he had offered one sacrifice for sins for ever, sat down on the right hand of God;

HEB 11:4... By faith Abel offered unto God a more excellent sacrifice than Cain, by which he obtained witness that he was righteous, God testifying of his gifts: and by it he being dead yet speaketh.

HEB 12:24... And to Jesus the mediator of the new covenant, and to the blood of sprinkling, that speaketh better things than that of Abel.

I stand with
Christ
Where do you stand?

MODERN JUDEO TEACHINGS	WORDS OF JESUS CHRIST
x JEWS are God's Chosen people.	✔JEWS are of their father the devil.
x Ye must be born again.	✔Ye must be born anothen (from above).
x Christ died for eveyone in the entire world.	✔I am not sent but unto the lost sheep of the House of Israel*.
x Everybody can make a decision to accept Christ to be saved and spend eternity in Heaven.	✔...except your righteousness shall exceed the righteousness of the scribes and Pharisees, ye shall in no case enter into the kingdom of heaven.
x We must go and preach the Gospel to all nations and races everywhere upon the entire earth.	✔Go not into the way of the Gentiles**, and into any city of the Samaritans enter ye not: But go rather to the lost sheep of the house of Israel*.
x If we run out of places in Israel* then it is OK to go elswhere and preach.	✔Ye shall not have gone over the cities of Israel*, till the Son of man be come.
x Anybody can be saved if they perform the right works.	✔No man can come to me, except the Father which hath sent me draw him:
x Follow our doctrine.	✔**Follow Me.**

*Israel in the Bible is "House of Jacob/Israel" family.

**Gentiles meaning any race or nation other than your own.

Printed in the United States
by Baker & Taylor Publisher Services